The Prestige

Trent 1

John Banks
Photography by G H F Atkins

© 2004 Venture Publications Ltd

ISBN 1 898432 83 X

Cover: An extremely rare colour view taken before the Second World War. A Huntingdon Street bus station, Nottingham, scene, it features a Weymann-bodied forward-entrance AEC Regent, No. **1026** (**RC 4632**) of 1937, and an unidentified single-decker.

Rear cover: From a batch of Midland Red-built SOS chassis of type SON, with 34-seat bodywork by Willowbrook, which were the last of many SOS chassis bought by Trent, No. **417** (**RC 7927**) has been preserved and restored by the Company. *(Geoff Coxon)*

Title page: A lovely portrait of No. **1056** (**RC 6005**), a Daimler COG5 dating from 1938. The bodywork to forward-entrance specification seating 54 was by Weymann, of Addlestone, and was of a style that had already appeared in the Trent fleet on some AEC Regents the previous year.

Opposite page and below: The Trent fleet was for a decade and a half from the mid twenties virtually synonymous with the SOS chassis, built by fellow BET company Midland Red. Loyalty to local coachbuilders was also a strong point, and most orders went to Brush Coachworks or Willowbrook. **RC 2715**, fleet number **315**, seen here in pristine, brand new condition, was a 1935 SOS DON with AEC 7.7-litre diesel engine and a Brush 34-seat saloon body. *(John Banks Collection)*

FOREWORD

The building blocks of today's Trent Motor Traction Company Limited were laid in the period covered by this book. Following its beginnings in 1913 the Company formed two critical masses around the cities of Derby and Nottingham shaped like two kidneys. The territory in between was largely taken up by Barton in the south and Midland General in the north save for services from Alfreton and Mansfield in the north and Derby to Nottingham in the middle. In 1925 the Company was floated on the London Stock Exchange and thus could then be considered to have come of age.

Everything described and illustrated in this book took place in a period that only its older readers will recall from personal experience, yet connections with today are there and are not so hard to find if the reader seeks them. When I joined Trent in 1968 at Nottingham, one of my conductors had started with the Company in 1924 - just eleven years after its formation; my office in Kent Street, Nottingham, was next to a small garage acquired in 1935 with the business of Dutton's Unity; in 2004 Trent still operates from garages at Belper, Hucknall and Nottingham built in the 1920s and 1930s; many current routes follow the pattern laid down in those days; an SOS single-decker is still owned; Derby bus station, a pleasing early thirties design, today struggles to cope with twelve-metre vehicles amid mixed public reaction to the news that it is to be demolished in favour of a modern facility.

Trent has touched the lives of many people over the last 90 years. Generations of the same families have travelled in its vehicles to school, to work, to the shops, to the cinema over the years and many have enjoyed a day trip to Skeggy and some the Grand Tour of Scotland. Thousands of people have given a lifetime of service to Trent: 45 and more years of service is not uncommon and a few have achieved 50.

As a management team my colleagues and I are proud of our Company's long history and achievements: we are but custodians equally of a legacy and a future as our centenary fast approaches. This book and its forthcoming companion Volume Two from Venture tell the story well through John Banks's text and the camera work of the legendary Geoffrey Atkins.

B R King, Managing Director
Trent Motor Traction Company Limited

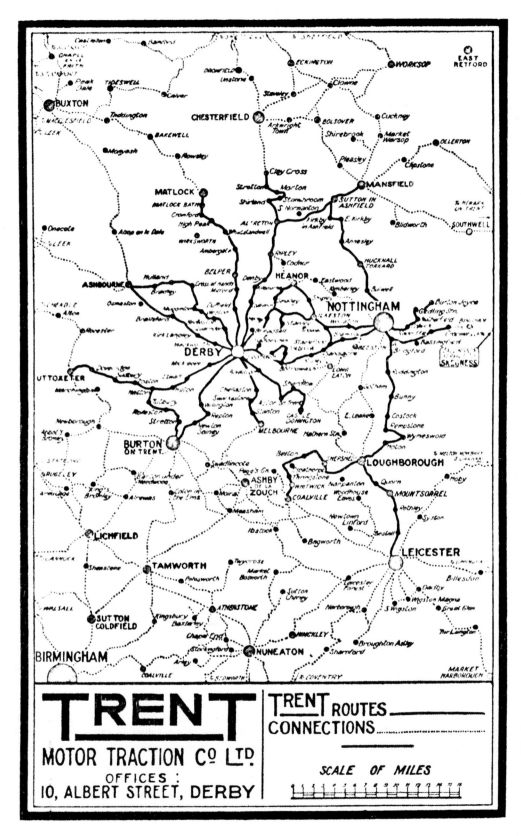

The Trent route system in the summer of 1924. *(John Banks Collection)*

INTRODUCTION

Rarely can the huntin', shootin' and fishin' brigade have been directly responsible for the formation of something so far removed from their daily round as a bus company. Yet this is how the forerunner of the Trent Motor Traction Company came into existence.

The British motor industry might today be practically non-existent, but such was not the case getting on for a hundred years ago, when among many names - some to fall by the wayside and some to flourish and become household names - that of Commercial Cars Ltd, of Luton, was prominent. The "Commer Car" owed its success to its reliability - many makes in those days were troublesome - but, even so, not as many were sold as had been hoped and in 1909 a separate concern, Commercial Car Hirers Ltd, was set up to make use of unsold vehicles by hiring them out.

These activities, relatively modest in themselves, gave rise to two companies that were to become household words - one internationally and the other in the Midlands of England. Commercial Cars Ltd surmounted some early difficulties and went on to become producer of the popular and successful Commer range of commercial and passenger chassis: an organisation that later passed into the Rootes group. Commercial Car Hirers Ltd - through that connection with "the gentry" - gave rise to the Trent Motor Traction Co. Ltd.

Commercial Car Hirers received an enquiry for a vehicle suited to carrying shooting parties on a Scottish landowner's estate. Once the vehicle, a 14-seater, was in use in Scotland, it was noticed with some interest by a guest who owned Osmaston Manor, near Ashbourne, in Derbyshire. That worthy thought that a similar vehicle would be useful for the conveyance of guests and staff at Osmaston and made

*One of the Commercial Car Hirers Ltd vehicles to pass to the new Company was this 1911 Commer, No. 9 (**LE 9601**). The Commer into Rootes Group transition for the chassis manufacturer was echoed by the bodybuilder, Scammell and Nephew, which became the equally well known Scammell Lorries Ltd, of Watford. LE 9601 was withdrawn by Trent in 1915. Points of interest include the driver's uniform, although the conductor apparently had none, and the passengers seated outside the saloon alongside the driving position. (John Banks Collection)*

arrangements to hire one from the same supplier.

The Derbyshire Commer Car was used to convey staff and guests from the Manor to Ashbourne and Derby and return and soon, in turn, attracted attention from other landowners, some of whom asked to borrow the vehicle. The demand was such that a second was acquired. It was found convenient to cancel the hiring arrangement and substitute a regular service running to a timetable between Derby and Ashbourne. At first the two Commers were garaged at the Green Man Hotel in Ashbourne.

Despite the opposition aroused by the new-fangled internal combustion engine at this time (just before the outbreak of the First World War: vehicles so powered had been practical for little more than a decade and some people had never seen one) in rural areas the venture was an instant success and attracted the attention of the British Electric Traction Company. A few years earlier, in 1905, the BET had been set up to promote tramway schemes. Somebody clearly realised that the "road motor" had a future, and the BET created a subsidiary - the British Automobile Development Co. Ltd - to look into questions relating to the carriage of passengers by such vehicles. The unfortunately chosen intials BAD became BAT through the substitution for the "D" for "Development" by "T" for "Traction" - and the British Automobile Traction Co. Ltd was born.

It was this concern that provided half of the capital of £20,000 - the other half coming from Commercial Car Hirers Ltd - in order that a new company might be set up to take over the services being run by the two Commers and to put in place a policy of expansion. Thus the Trent Motor Traction Co. Ltd was registered on 31st October 1913 and services under its aegis started the following 3rd November. Routes operated by Commercial Car Hirers at the time of the transfer were:

Derby - Ashbourne (Mon - Sat)
Derby - Alfreton
Derby - Uttoxeter (Mon - Sat)
Derby - Melbourne (Sats only)
Alfreton - Chesterfield (Mon - Sat)
Clay Cross - Tupton - Chesterfield (Not Suns & Weds)

Six vehicles had been in use for this work and all passed to Trent. Garaging had become established at Alfreton but the new Company turned to Derby for its headquarters, setting up initially in London Road and later Uttoxeter New Road.

The first vehicles new to Trent were six more Commers in January 1914. Despite the close connection with Commer, the next new buses, in February - July 1914, were twelve Maudslays, required for an ambitious programme of expansion. An early success was to beat Chesterfield Corporation, at that time developing its own bus services, onto the road between Chesterfield and Staveley, though the Corporation were soon running in opposition.

All the young Company's plans were set at naught, however, as were those of most other motor lorry and bus proprietors, by the outbreak on 4th August 1914 of what came to be known as the First World War. There had been a very strong traditionalist core of opinion in the military that the war could, and would, be won by cavalry and, indeed, there would be examples of mounted troops facing tanks. Some less hidebound strategists, however, realised that mechanised warfare was the way forward. An immediate result of this was the arrival of requisition notices from the War Office and by early 1915 the Trent fleet stood at two, both in need of overhaul. A vehicle was hired from the Potteries Electric Traction Company (PET, later PMT), but relief was short-lived as that, too, was soon requisitioned.

Services clearly suffered: became, in fact, virtually non-existent; Trent was able to place orders for new Tilling-Stevens chassis, a make that the military considered too complicated, with its petrol-electric transmission in place of the conventional clutch and gearbox. The petrol-electric system was very reliable and smooth in operation, but it needed skilled maintenance staff with specialist training. From the spring of 1915 these new vehicles enabled services to be built up again.

The war years, however, brought Trent its fair share of difficulties. Maintenance of the vehicles, or lack of it, resulting in non-availability of buses and high petrol consumption when they were available, gave particular cause for concern. This was partially alleviated when the services were obtained, on

*This early official view is of interest in illustrating, as the centre of three Birch-bodied Trent vehicles, No. **D103** (**CH 1209**), one of the first four replacement Tilling Stevens TS3 chassis delivered in April 1915, seen here as rebodied circa 1920/1. It is flanked by **TS 2566**, fleet number unknown, a similar TS3 but with char-à-bancs coachwork, new in 1920; and 1921 Vulcan **V143** (**CH 2786**). (John Banks Collection)*

an occasional consultancy basis, of L G Wyndham-Shire of the Birmingham and Midland Motor Omnibus Company. Trent was to have a long and fruitful association with BMMO.

Another serious problem was what were perceived as excessive charges levied, albeit legally, by local authorities on Trent towards maintenance of roads along which the Company's services passed.

Competition on the Derby to Ashbourne road did nothing to help matters, and in 1917 one J Harrison, of Ashbourne, who had run in opposition to Trent and CCHL before them, was bought out, no doubt amicably, for he was kept on as Trent's Ashbourne agent.

About shortages of petrol very little could be done, other than to cut out unnecessary or little-used journeys, and by seeking alternative fuels. Another neighbouring operator again came to Trent's aid, when Barton Brothers, of Beeston, supplied a roof-mounted gas bag, which allowed the bus to which it was fitted to run on coal gas. After trials further bags were purchased, although not from Barton, and coal gas was drawn as required from standards rented from Derby Corporation. By the end of 1917, about one third of the Company's service

mileage was worked by gas-power. Even so, approximately 1,500 miles per month of scheduled mileage was being lost and under such circumstances very little could be done by way of expansion.

In 1917 the first Trent timetable appeared, followed by a second issue, complete with map, the following year. With Derby at the centre, services radiated outwards along the main roads to Ashbourne, Belper, Alfreton, Spondon, Borrowash, Melbourne and Burton. Some two dozen or more villages off these main roads were optimistically shown on the map, but the buses did not serve them directly: inhabitants thereof had to walk to the main road.

The end of hostilities, though bringing its own set of problems of supply and austerity, nonetheless allowed consolidation and some confident forward planning. The Commers had all gone by the end of 1919 and more Tilling-Stevens chassis were ordered. The latter make was in the majority, though joined by some Vulcans, Thornycrofts and Daimlers, until the Company turned to the BMMO-built SOS chassis as its standard in 1925: a standard that pertained through to the late 1930s, when AECs and Daimlers became the norm.

Like many of the other operators having the financial backing of the BAT, Trent was able to pursue a steady policy of buying out other operators; the latter were frequently under-capitalised and had little choice but to sell. Trent started in a small way with three single vehicle acquisitions, including the aforementioned Harrison, before 1920. Thereafter the momentum increased and throughout the twenties and thirties many independent operators were absorbed.

One of the early acquisitions was that of the Loughborough Road Car Co. Ltd, which was small and in financial difficulties; the single vehicle taken over was never used by Trent. Nonetheless the transaction was an important one in that it led to Trent's expansion into Leicester with a service to that city from Loughborough.

Other important towns and cities were reached in turn and the Company's vehicles were seen in Nottingham from 1919; by agreement with the BMMO the Company was able to run into Burton on Trent and in 1920 a Derby to Bakewell service commenced.

Expansion thereafter, both as to services operated and vehicles purchased to operate them, was considerable. Despite its successes, the Company had rivals both large and small and in the 1920s competition was fierce. Public demand for bus services was intense and many survivors of the recent war had gained therein some experience with mechanically propelled vehicles. Once back home, and looking for a way to make a living in the "land fit for heroes", not a few such men began to run a bus. Some stayed the course for a while and their fleets grew. This brought about a curious situation that reversed the idea of "one law for the rich and another for the poor" in that when the small operator ran his vehicle a minute or two ahead of Trent on an established service, it was hailed as free enterprise, yet when Trent returned the compliment, there were cries of "Foul".

Although under-capitalised and with no "big company" support, the Loughborough Road Car Company turned out vehicles that looked impressive and belied the humble status of their owner. This 1913/4 Frank Searle-designed Daimler CC had gone before the sale to Trent: the single vehicle acquired by the latter - though never used and immediately sold - was a Tilling-Stevens. (John Banks Collection)

Despite all that, the Company prospered and still exists in the new Millennium. The pages that follow will attempt, mainly through the work of Geoffrey Atkins, to illustrate the vehicles Trent has used: up to the end of the Second World War in this first volume and from then onwards in Volume Two. Unless indicated otherwise, all photographs were taken by G H F Atkins and are copyright the John Banks Collection.

Valued and much appreciated assistance has once again come from Ron Maybray over early vehicle details; David Bean and Alan Oxley have read and checked the text - to its undoubted benefit; Dave and Mary Shaw have read the proofs. Grateful thanks to all: the writer is ever in your debt.

Readers are cautioned that this book does not claim to present either a definitive history or a full fleet list. For that, the two books on the Company by David Bean, published in 1998 (Volume One) and 2002 (Volume Two) by Robin Hood Publishing, are strongly recommended.

John Banks
Romiley, Cheshire
May 2004

Above: An enthusiastic party of 29 plus the driver had filled to capacity the 29-seat *char-à-bancs* body on No. **55** (**CH 1314**). The Tilling-Stevens TS3 chassis dated from 1915 and had originally carried a Brush 28-seat saloon body and the registration number CH 1276. *(John Banks Collection)*

Below: Number **D119**, another Tilling-Stevens TS3, started life in 1919 registered CH 1620, later becoming **CH 1600**. To add to the confusion, the 28-seat Brush body had originally been carried by No. D106 (CH 1287). Further renumbered as 102 by the end of 1926, the vehicle was withdrawn in 1929. *(John Banks Collection)*

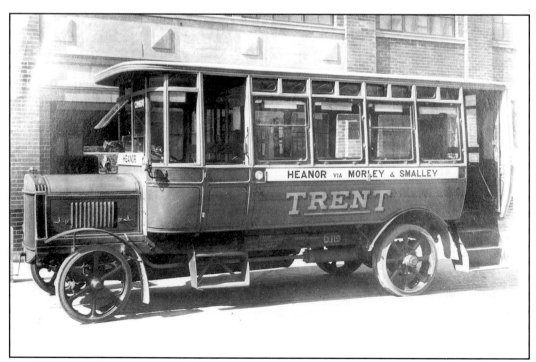

Above: **CH 1834** was a 1920 example of the Tilling-Stevens TS3 model, which started out with the fleet number **D128**; it was later renumbered 130, 769 and 900. Converted as a B1 model by the end of 1929, it lasted in Trent service until 1933. The Holmes bodywork had 28 seats. *(John Banks Collection)*

Below: Seen outside the Trent premises in Loughborough (earlier used by the Loughborough Road Car Company) waiting to leave on the Nottingham service is No. **D124** (**CH 1769**); it had similar Holmes bodywork but little is known about its history after delivery into the Trent fleet in 1920. *(John Banks Collection)*

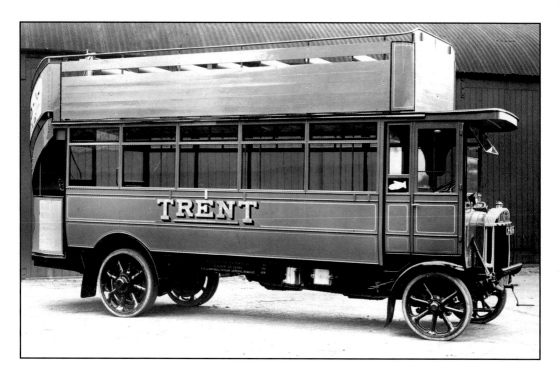

Above and below: By 1924 the Tilling-Stevens model was the TS6. Trent took delivery of 20: ten each single- and double-deck; they all had Brush bodywork. Number **204** (**CH 4066**) epitomises the open-top bodywork and the solid-tyred wheels when brand new. A seating capacity of 57 was rather high for that period. All twenty were converted in 1928 to run on pneumatic tyres. In these views taken before delivery, the livery was the light red of the BET - the first Trent buses to be so turned out. *(Both: John Banks Collection)*

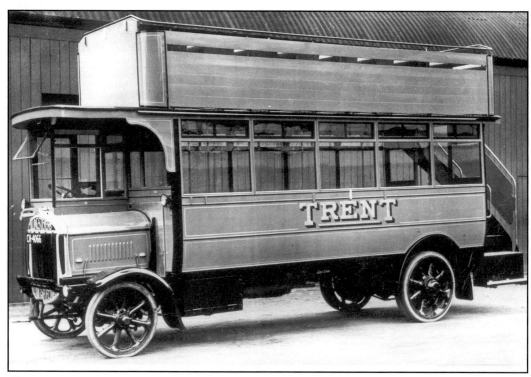

Above and below: There was a time when a high percentage of buses withdrawn from passenger-carrying service passed to travelling fairground showmen and saw out their days hauling prodigious loads, more often than not towing multiple trailers, and providing power for the various funfair equipment. Vehicles fitted with petrol-electric transmission, as were the Tilling-Stevens models for many years, were particularly useful, as the electric motors could be used to drive the roundabouts directly, instead of the vehicle's engine, or an auxiliary mounted inside, driving a generator. **CH 4072** *(above)* had been Trent No. 204, one of the 57-seat double-deckers, whereas **CH 4077**, formerly No. 301 *(below)*, was always a single-decker. The Brush bodywork had seated 37 when in Trent service. They both gained pneumatic tyres in 1928 and were withdrawn by Trent in February 1932 (CH 4072) and September 1931.

Above: Another well-filled outing: 28 passengers this time, and the driver is missing. The gentleman alongside with the braces and shiny shoes could be he. The vehicle is No. **53**, a 1920 Tilling-Stevens TS3 with Birch 29-seat coachwork, registered **KN 8686**, which had carried the fleet number D139 when new. The renumbering to 53 took place before the end of 1926 but was probably quite early in the vehicle's life with Trent if its pristine condition - indeed, it looks new - in this picture is any guide. The vehicle was withdrawn in 1930. *(John Banks Collection)*

Below: Between almost total reliance on the products of Tilling-Stevens and the switch to Midland Red-built SOS chassis there were a number of Vulcans, Thornycrofts and Daimlers. One of the latter was No. **810** (**CH 4856**), a 31-seater with Ransomes saloon bodywork, delivered in 1925. Later rebodied, again as a 31-seater, with an ex-Midland Red body, the bus was withdrawn in 1933. Its chassis and body were separated and sold to different purchasers. *(John Banks Collection)*

Above: The great Trent switch to SOS chassis built by fellow BET member Midland Red (the fleetname of the Birmingham and Midland Motor Omnibus Company) began modestly in 1925 with a pair of S models, Nos 900/1, registered CH 4947/6. Saloon bodywork with 31 seats was by Ransomes. Number 900 was, then, the first of them all according to the fleet numbers, but in this view **CH 4947** was carrying its 1930 renumbering **711**. In the same year it was converted as an SOS ODD type and rebodied, almost certainly by Midland Red at Carlyle Works, using United, of Lowestoft, parts as a 26-seater. It is illustrated thus in this October 1933 picture at Huntingdon Street, Nottingham, and was withdrawn in 1936.

Below: More S models arrived in 1926, including No. **919** (**CH 5430**); in this manufacturer's photograph the original Ransomes 31-seat bodywork is illustrated. This bus underwent conversion and rebodying as described above for CH 4947 (a total of 21 was so dealt with) and was also renumbered into the 700 series and withdrawn in 1936. *(John Banks Collection)*

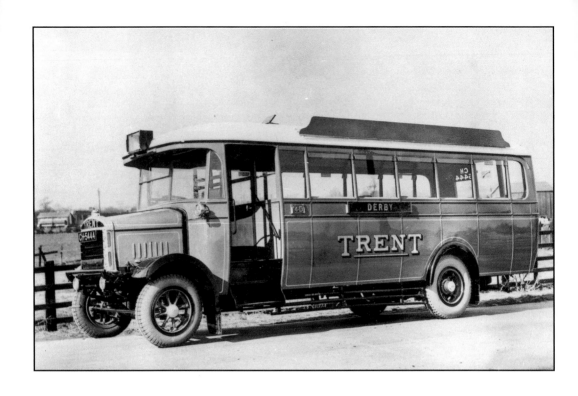

Above and below: Eleven more of the SOS S models dating from 1926 were also converted to ODD specification, but in 1931. Their new bodies - by Brush - were virtually identical to those constructed using United parts in 1930. These were also renumbered into the 700 series and withdrawn in 1936. Many of the original bodies from the 1930/1 conversions were reused on earlier chassis of Tilling-Stevens or Daimler manufacture. Number **724** (**CH 5444**) - originally fleet number 924 - is illustrated in 1931 having just been fitted with its new Brush body. *(Both: John Banks Collection)*

Above: In a quiet early thirties scene in Sitwell Street, Spondon, Trent No. **716** (**CH 5438**) waits to leave for Derby. Originally a Ransomes-bodied 31-seater, this 1926 SOS S model had been rebodied by Midland Red with United components, as described on page 15. The vehicle was parked alongside a "Trent Parcel Service Agent" sign, which doubtless doubled as a bus stop. *(John Banks Collection)*

Below: In July 1931, despite its "Skegness is Bracing" proclamation, No. **731** (**CH 5453**) was going to Wilford Hill on service 31. This was another of the eleven rebodied in 1931 as 26-seaters by Brush. These five had had bodies from the Daimler CMs when new; the latter having been converted to *char-à-bancs* specification.

Above and below: In 1927 the SOS Q model with forward-control driver-beside-engine layout was introduced into the Trent fleet. This design allowed a higher seating capacity and the Brush saloon bodywork was for 37. Twenty-five Qs were delivered during the year and all lasted into the 1940s, some as far as 1945. Eight were converted for use as ambulances during the war. In the upper picture No. **954** (**CH 6234**) is seen in 1932 at Huntingdon Street with its Brush bodywork in original condition. A year or so later No. **957** (**CH 6238**) *(below)* displays a somewhat smoother outline after its original body had been rebuilt by the Company. Both pictures are at Huntingdon Street, Nottingham, scene of so many of Geoffrey Atkins's memorable coachwork portraits.

Above: In 1927 there were also five SOS QC model all-weather coaches with Carlyle 30-seat bodies. The first of them, No. **600** (**CH 6256**), had ventured as far as Land's End without the benefit of brakes fitted to the front wheels, as is evident from this photograph recording the occasion. Although the roads were quieter then, the anachronistic rear-wheel-brakes-only specification would not survive for much longer. All five were withdrawn in 1936. *(John Banks Collection)*

Below: Every now and again some thought has to be given whether to include an example of Geoffrey Atkins's very early photography. Operating as he was, as an impecunious teenager, with a modest camera, the occasional exposure fell short of the high standards he was even then setting himself. His notes on the back of the original of this illustration are interesting and tipped the scales towards inclusion: "Photo taken with a Vest Pocket Kodak. Bus No. 960. The regular Nottingham - Skegness bus. Note Trent Daimler bus in the background, Parliament Street Bridge was the City terminus at that time." The photograph was taken in June 1929 in Parliament Street, Nottingham. Number **960** was **CH 6242**, one of the 1927 SOS Qs. Apart from the Trent interest, the picture is worth having for the portrait of the motorcycle combination pilot, chugging along hand out and helmetless.

Above: For 1928 the SOS model changed to the QL, still with 37-seat bodywork, the order for which was split between Brush and Ransomes. Number **523** (**CH 7753**) was one of the Brush examples, with a small supporting bracket at the top of the forward door pillar.

Below: The Ransomes version had a larger supporting bracket: although there were other minor detail differences, this bracket was the quick way of telling which manufacturer had built the body. There were 38 of these 1928 SOS QLs and all had gone by the end of 1937. Illustrated is No. **533** (**CH 7709**).

Above: In July 1929 Geoffrey Atkins was on his way to Skegness on holiday. Travelling by Trent, he was well placed to photograph his transport at the refreshment stop at Langworth, Lincolnshire. The George Refreshment Rooms and Garage form a backdrop for brand new SOS M model No. **416** (**CH 8109**), in service since the preceding May. Bodywork was to 34-seat saloon specification by Short Brothers, of Rochester. This vehicle was converted as an ambulance in 1939 and finally withdrawn in 1945.

Below: A closer view of No. **416** showing the "LIMITED STOP SERVICE SKEGNESS" route board. The narrow cab, into which the engine did not protrude, is evident.

Above: Exactly a year later the photographer was again *en route*, this time towards home after a holiday in bracing Skegness, and again the camera came out at the Langworth refreshment stop. The leading vehicle is No. **405** (**CH 8111**), another 1929 SOS M 34-seater, bound for Derby. The vehicle behind, an SOS Q, was going to Nottingham and was doubtless the photographer's transport on this occasion. Just visible at the extreme right of the picture is another SOS M, No. **417** (**CH 8110**), with its emergency door open.

Below and >> opposite page: Another aspect of the Skegness holiday season is seen in these busy August 1931 scenes at Huntingdon Street, Nottingham. Holidaymakers are waiting to board Trent vehicles, one of which, No. **604** (**CH 6260**), was the last of the 1927 batch of five SOS QC 30-seaters. A Trent employee is loading luggage into one of the Company's vans and although the sun was not yet out no doubt expectations were high.

<< *Opposite page:* Three imposing SOS QLC types were delivered among all the QLs in 1928. Nos 650-2 (CH 7144/6/5) had all-weather coachwork by Short Brothers. Number **652** (**CH 7145**) was photographed at the Lawn Motor Park, Skegness, in July 1929.

Above: Number **537** (**CH 7706**), one of the Ransomes-bodied 1928 SOS QLs, was photographed in as-built condition before delivery to Trent. *(John Banks Collection)*

Below: An early shot of a similar vehicle: No. **516** (**CH 7702**) was about a year old when caught parked in the centre of the road - the usual stance for buses at that time - in Trinity Square, Nottingham, in August 1929.

SOS M type No. 419 (CH 8114), new in 1929, features in an evocative October 1934 night scene at Huntingdon Street as it waits to leave for Hucknall. A Barton Leyland Lion stands alongside.

Close colleague in the numbering system No. **421** (**CH 8118**) is seen at Huntingdon Street in April 1933.

Above: In a May 1935 scene at Stockwell Gate, Mansfield, No. **206** (**CH 8906**) represents the Brush-bodied 34-seat SOS COD saloons delivered in 1930. The vehicle had carried fleet number 456 when new in 1930 and was renumbered 206 in 1932. Along with many other vehicles of the same type it was impressed by the military in 1940 and worked under Northern Command at York. It later ran for Midland Red.

Below: A similar vehicle with a similar history, seen at Huntingdon Street in April 1935. **CH 8912** had been fleet number 462 when new and was renumbered **212** in 1932.

Above: Doubtless spirits were as damp as the weather as these hopeful holidaymakers waited to board Trent's 1930 SOS COD type No. **465 (CH 8915)** at Huntingdon Street on a Saturday in August 1931. The vehicle was renumbered 215 in 1932 and was another of the 15 (Nos 200-6/8-13/5/6) to pass to Northern Command in 1940. It was not, however, one of the ten (201/2/4-6/10-3/6) that went on to work in the Midland Red fleet.

Below: The same vehicle in a different part of the same bus station about three years later. By the time of this picture **CH 8915** had been renumbered (in 1932) as **215**.

Above: The all-weather coach fleet was augmented with a trio of SOS QLCs in 1930. Short Brothers 30-seat coachwork was fitted. Representing CH 8918-20 (672/0/1) at Huntingdon Street in 1934 was No. **671** (**CH 8920**). All three were withdrawn in 1937.

Below: This splendidly animated scene at Huntingdon Street records Trent's practice of hiring coaches to cope with the rush to the coast at summer weekends. Norfolk Motor Services Ltd, of Great Yarmouth, had provided a pair of Crossley Alphas fitted with Eaton 32-seat coachwork, and they are seen being loaded for the return to that resort. In a scene not too often depicted with such character, the driver is on the roof stowing luggage and suitcases are being handed up while passengers stand around waiting to board. Number **14** (**EX 2684**) had been new in July 1930; its companion was No. **15**, confusingly registered **EX 2865**, which had been delivered in May 1931 although its chassis number was only twelve higher than that of EX 2684. Geoffrey Atkins's original print has no details attached, but the condition of the vehicles suggests that this was probably the summer of 1931. The Crossleys were sold in 1941; both found new owners and later ran for fairground showmen in the early postwar period.

Above: By 1931, in comparison with the products of AEC and Leyland, the SOS profile was beginning to look a little dated, not helped by the insistence on that narrow driving cab. Examples of the IM6 six-cylinder- and IM4 four-cylinder-engined models were bought for the Trent fleet in that year. The IM4 is exemplified by No. **227** (**CH 9923**), photographed in August 1934.

Below: In this group, taken at Huntingdon Street in June 1935, the centre vehicle is one of the 1931 IM6s, No. **133** (**CH 9913**). Alongside for comparison is an IM4, No. **229** (**CH 9925**), and next to the railings is No. **419** (**CH 8114**), a 1929 SOS M type. Bodywork on the 1934 IM4s and IM6s was to 34-seat saloon specification by Short Brothers.

Above: It is never easy to resist including Geoffrey Atkins's superlative night scenes in these compilations. This particularly atmospheric example, again from an undated original, was probably taken in 1934. About to depart for Hucknall, Trent's No. **479** (**CH 9925**), a 1931 SOS IM4 Short Brothers-bodied 34-seater, waits in the rain at Huntingdon Street alongside a Nottingham AEC Regent, No. **13** (**TV 733**) of 1930.

Below: Brand new No. **253** (**RC 538**), as delivered in July 1932. An SOS IM4, it had 34-seat bodywork by Brush. Note the Trent practice of applying the legal owner lettering on the safety guardrails instead of the body panels.

Above: Nineteen-thirty-two's saloons again comprised some of both IM4 and IM6 types: 25 of the former and ten of the latter. Representing the six-cylinder machines, at Huntingdon Street in July 1935, was the last of the batch, No. **145** (**RC 910**), which had been new in October 1932. The 34-seat bodywork was by Short Brothers. This and eight more of the ten survived in the Trent fleet until 1948 (No. 140 went in 1940).

Below: A fine action shot of 1933 SOS IM4 No. **265** (**CH 1284**) at Huntingdon Street/King Edward Street, Nottingham, in 1934. This vehicle was fitted with a Gardner 4-cylinder diesel engine: its performance on the road to Derby, especially on the hills, would thus have been far from lively.

<< *Opposite page and above:* The SOS ON type was introduced in 1934 to take advantage of the maximum legal vehicle-length of 27ft 6ins. Trent took a batch of 12 with Duple rear-entrance bodywork for "dual-purpose" use. The batch was Nos 680-91 (RC 1800-11), and we illustrate No. **689** (**RC 1809**) at Huntingdon Street and No. **683** (**RC 1803**) at Lower Mosley Street, Manchester, respectively in July and September 1934. The vehicles had been in service since the previous June.

Below: Duple also supplied the 31-seat coach bodies on six SOS ON models in 1935, typified in as-built condition by No. **630** (**RC 2551**) about six weeks after its March 1935 entry into service.

Above: In 1935 the first SOS DON models arrived in the Trent fleet. The DON was an ON with an AEC 7.7-litre diesel engine in place of the BMMO RR2LB petrol unit. Number **324** (**RC 2724**) was one of 30 delivered in that year, all with Brush bodies; half were 34- and half 36-seaters. Number 324 was photographed at Gedling in October 1935 when just over three months old. All 30 lasted well into the postwar period, being withdrawn between 1950 and 1953.

Below: A further 40 DONs came in 1936, needed to replace the mixed vehicle intake from acquired operators. All had Brush 36-seat bodywork and a typical example was No. **353** (**RC 3724**), a June 1936 delivery that lasted until 1953. This picture gives a good view of the cast TRENT nameplate fixed to the stair riser in the entrance. Twenty of this batch (not including No. 353) were rebodied by Willowbrook in 1949, lasting thence until 1958.

Above: Number **329** (**RC 2729**), the last of the thirty 1935 SOS DONs, despite its 14 years, was turned out on the Derby to Manchester express service on 23rd July 1949. It is seen here loading at Manchester for the return to Derby. *(John Banks Collection/Keith Healey)*

Below: The second of that same batch, No. **301** (**RC 2701**), was photographed at Derby Cattle Market in May 1951, looking far less than its age. The longevity achieved by this 1935 vehicle was aided by some rebuilding work carried out by the Company, evident in the slightly smoother profile. This was one of seven of the batch to last into 1953 in Trent service. After withdrawal it was sold to a dealer in November 1953 and scrapped.

Above: The 1934 batch of Duple-bodied SOS ON types, Nos 680-91 (RC 1800-11), were fitted with AEC 7.7-litre diesel engines, in place of their original SOS petrol engines, and Willowbrook 35-seat front-entrance saloon bodies in place of the Duple dual-purpose units, in 1946. This transformation caused a renumbering to 370-81 and, in 1949, they were again renumbered as 500-11. The Willowbrook bodies were true half-cabs: although the engine protruded into the cab area, there was more room at arm level than had been the case with the narrower cabs on the original bodies. Number **506** (**RC 1806**) was at Derby bus station in September 1949.

Below: The nearside aspect of the transformed 1934 vehicles is provided by No. **504** (**RC 1804**) at Huntingdon Street in May 1951. These two vehicles were withdrawn in 1955 and No. 504 survived with a builder - Davis, of Winsford - until 1959, when it was scrapped. It had last been licensed in April 1958.

In March 1935 ten 1926 SOS FS types, not otherwise represented in the Trent fleet, were hired from Midland Red and subsequently purchased. With the change of name rather crudely brought about, **HA 3583** was at Huntingdon Street a month later, still with Midland Red fleet number **583**. It became Trent 808 and was withdrawn in 1936. All ten had gone from passenger service by the end of 1937.

Above: The ex-Midland Red 1926 SOS FS types acquired by Trent in 1935 were from a relatively early development stage of Midland Red-built vehicles and by the mid 1930s were antiquated in appearance compared with new vehicles from the same manufacturer then entering service with Trent. The picture above graphically illustrates the advances - and they were advances in specification as well as in appearance. Apart from the "rather less than half"-cab, No. **307** (**RC 2707**), an AEC-engined SOS DON/Brush 36-seater of 1935, was a world apart from the 1926 FS, despite the less than a decade between them. The prominent cast TRENT nameplate affixed to the radiator header-tank and the SOS emblem are of interest. *(John Banks Collection)*

Above: One of the ten ex-Midland Red SOS FS models (No. 801, registered HA 3553) was destroyed by fire in 1936; eight of the remainder found new owners, though it is not known if any were PSV operators; and one was retained by Trent for use as a driver-training vehicle. Number 802 (**HA 3573**) was converted to fully fronted specification and was fitted with an extra set of controls, including a second steering wheel, on the nearside. As renumbered **15**, it is seen at Derby in September 1949.

Below: The nearside-rear angle of No. **15** (**HA 3573**) shows that the Brush bodywork was largely unaltered behind the entrance although it is believed not to have retained a full set of seats. The picture was taken in the same month, but at Huntingdon Street. No. 15 was withdrawn in 1953.

41

Above: With effect from 9th June 1935, the business of Retford Coachways Ltd was jointly taken over by East Midland Motor Services, the Lincolnshire Road Car Company and Trent. Two Retford vehicles passed into the Trent fleet: an AEC Regal and the 1932 Albion Victor DH49 illustrated. The 20-seat bodywork on **VO 7858** was by Taylor. Seen here still in Retford Coachways livery, the vehicle became Trent's No. 1201.

Below: An important acquisition, with effect from 1st November 1935, was of Dutton's Unity Services Ltd, of Nottingham. Sixteen vehicles - three GMCs, six Tilling-Stevens, three AEC Regals and four Dennis Lancets, passed to Trent. An earlier Dutton vehicle that did not was **GE 9615**, a four-cylinder Albion forward-control chassis fitted with bodywork by the chassis-builder. The vehicle was photographed outside Dutton's Kent Street, Nottingham, premises in September 1933.

Above: The Dutton's Unity vehicle that was to become Trent fleet number 1211 was **ATV 301**, a 1934 Dennis Lancet with Willowbrook 36-seat saloon bodywork. In this view it was brand new and awaiting delivery to Dutton, with whom it would have a very short life before adopting Trent livery. *(John Banks Collection)*

Below: Another Dennis Lancet, a close contemporary of ATV 301, was registered **ATV 4**. It would, soon after this picture was taken, be numbered 1212 in the Trent fleet. Again bodied by Willowbrook, it was a 32-seat coach. This is a Kent Street picture, from the summer of 1935. The agreement to buy Dutton's was dated 28th August 1935; the picture was taken in that month so it is just possible that the vehicle was legally in Trent ownership.

Above: Seen here in May 1934 before the Trent takeover, AEC Regal 4 **TV 8971** would the following year become Trent fleet number 1215. Brand new in this picture, it was fitted with Brush 32-seat front-entrance saloon bodywork. As renumbered by Trent (No. 1204), it lasted in service with the Company until 1940. It passed to Hulley, of Baslow, was rebodied by Burlingham and was not withdrawn until 1955.

Below: Dutton's **TV 7472** was a 1932 Tilling-Stevens B49A7 model, with Willowbrook 32-seat bodywork. As Trent No. 1217 (soon renumbered 1213) it was withdrawn in 1936. It later ran for Safeguard, of Guildford, but was withdrawn and scrapped in 1938. Another August 1935 photograph at Kent Street.

Above: Trent No. **1202** (**ATO 209**) had been No. 1213 when taken over from Dutton's Unity. It was an AEC Regal 4, with Willowbrook 32-seat front-entrance service bus bodywork with the unusual feature of lacking a canopy over the bonnet. It ran for Trent until 1940. *(John Banks Collection)*

Below: Four vehicles were acquired from R E Horspool, of Loughborough, on 15th December 1935, including **JU 3060** (later Trent 1235 and then 1228). This was a 1933 Dennis Lancet bodied as a 32-seater by Willowbrook. After withdrawn by Trent it was sold, in January 1947, to the South Notts Bus Co. Ltd, of Gotham, as their fleet number 33.

<< *Opposite page:* There had been no double-deckers in the fleet for some time prior to the arrival of a batch of 15 SOS FEDD models in 1936. Metro-Cammell 56-seat front-entrance metal-framed bodywork was fitted. Originally petrol-engined, using the SOS RR2LB unit, they were in 1943 fitted with AEC 7.7-litre diesel engines. A gleaming No. **1011** (**RC 3333**) was at Huntingdon Street in September 1936.

Above: One of the 1936 SOS DONs from the 20 that were not rebodied, No. **330** (**RC 3701**), is seen in postwar condition at Derby in September 1949. It was withdrawn in 1953 and passed via a dealer to a showman. It is recorded as still working thus in 1962.

Below: The next vehicle in the sequence, and obviously another not to have been rebodied, was a 1951 withdrawal and also ended up with a showman, a Mr Hodges, of Coventry. **RC 3702**, the former Trent No. 331, is seen at the Nottingham Goose Fair in October 1955 with windows panelled over but otherwise retaining its bus outline. The vehicle was later scrapped in Birmingham.

Above: For its single-deck service saloons in 1937 Trent switched its allegiance to the Associated Equipment Co. Ltd and ordered a batch of 20 Regal chassis. The order for 35-seat front-entrance bodywork was split equally between Duple and Willowbrook. A Duple example was No. **703** (**RC 4604**), seen here in Nottingham in 1953 having undergone some rebuilding (in 1948) by the Company. It was withdrawn in 1955 and later ran for a contractor, being scrapped in 1961.

Below: AEC Regal No. **711** (**RC 4612**) was one of the Willowbrook-bodied vehicles, seen here in a picture taken opposite Derby bus station in September 1949. It was fitted with a new body, also by Willowbrook, in 1950 and was a 1958 withdrawal; it is alleged to have survived in the hands of a dealer until at least April 1967.

Above: When the 1926 ex-Midland Red SOS FS, No. 15, which had been in use as a dual-control driver-trainer *(see page 41)*, finally had to be pensioned off, it was replaced with one of the 1936 SOS DONs. **RC 3734**, which had been fleet number 363, was converted in much the same way, with a fully fronted double cab and full dual controls and it took the same fleet number, **15**. The two steering wheels are clearly visible in this Derby bus station view of September 1957. The vehicle was sold to a dealer in October 1960 and then to a showman.

Below: Here is one of the twenty 1936 DONs that were rebodied by Willowbrook as 35-seaters *(see page 36)* in 1949. Number **512** (formerly 332), registered **RC 3703**, was at Derby in May 1952.

Soon after its rebodying by Willowbrook, the former No. 362, now **528** (**RC 3733**), was at Huntingdon Street in August 1949. Withdrawn in 1958, it later ran briefly for a Stockport contractor.

Sixteen of the twenty 1937 AEC Regals were rebodied as 35-seaters by Willowbrook in 1950, epitomised by No. **700** (**RC 4601**), the first of the batch, at Buxton in August 1951.

Thirty AEC Regents also came in 1937, fitted with Weymann 54-seat front-entrance bodies. Numbers **1035/27 (RC 4641/33)** were heading into Nottingham, complete with wartime blackout aids and masked nearside headlamps (the bulbs would have been removed from the offside lamps), at Mansfield Road, Nottingham, in March 1940.

Above: AEC Regent No. **1029** (**RC 4635**) in postwar condition at Huntingdon Street in August 1947. In 1949 this vehicle would be rebodied as a lowbridge 55-seater by Willowbrook. The two buses on the previous page were also rebodied as lowbridge vehicles. In all, 29 of the 30 were rebodied.

Below: From a deteriorating negative, caught only just in time by modern digital preservation, local lads are pictured frolicking in the snow as AEC Regent/MCCW No. **1025** (**RC 4631**) gently makes its way along Mansfield Road, Nottingham, at the junction with Hucknall Road. It was on service 62 to Mansfield and the picture was taken during the war. The vehicle was rebodied to highbridge specification by Willowbrook after the war, retaining its original number until 1957, when it was renumbered 1163.

Upper: All except No. 1036, which was withdrawn in 1947, of the 1937 batch of 30 AEC Regents were rebodied by Willowbrook in 1948/9, 22 as lowbridge and 7 as highbridge. This caused a renumbering and **RC 4645** (originally No. 1039), was now lowbridge No. **1349** at Granby Street, Nottingham, in January 1951.

Centre: The highbridge rebodies were not renumbered, not having changed their specification, although in 1957 the seven were brought together as Nos 1162-8. In August 1949, No. **1043** (**RC 4649**), with its new Willowbrook highbridge body fitted in 1948, was at Huntingdon Street, standing next to an apparently abandoned suitcase. All seven of the highbridge rebodies were withdrawn in 1958: the lowbridge vehicles lasted a year or so longer.

Lower: Trent No. 1330 (**RC 4624**), one of the lowbridge rebodies, found further work with Central Coaches, of Uppingham, after withdrawal in 1960. It had been sold by Trent to the dealer Cowley, of Salford, but was probably sold on by Cowley to this new owner fairly local to Trent without ever having travelled to and from Lancashire. (*Geoff Coxon*)

Above: The Company's need to hire vehicles to help with summer holiday traffic increased as the thirties progressed. Nottingham Corporation's 1929 AEC Reliance No. **82** (**MY 539**) found itself pressed on to Trent's Doncaster service one Saturday in July 1936. The photograph was taken at Huntingdon Street. Once again Geoffrey Atkins has captured some characterful cameos of passengers standing around waiting to board.

Below: In this August 1938 scene, another at Huntingdon Street, three Leyland Lions - two LT7s (**BNN 716/7**) and an LT5B (**ANN 830**) - from the Wass Brothers, of Mansfield, fleet were working for Trent. All three were showing "PRIVATE" in the destination screens, but with suitcases in the roof-mounted luggage-racks they were almost certainly bound for the coast - probably Skegness.

Above: The favoured manufacturer for double-deck chassis changed to Daimler in 1938, when 15 COG5s with Weymann highbridge bodywork were delivered. A further twelve came in 1939, of which No. **1071** (**RC 7082**) is illustrated in August 1948 carrying an all-over red livery. The bodywork had been rebuilt by Willowbrook in 1946.

Below: Number **1055** (**RC 6004**) was one of the 1938 Daimler COG5s, seen here in an early postwar Huntingdon Street scene. Fourteen of this batch were rebodied - six by Willowbrook and eight by Brush - in 1946 and 1948 respectively. Number 1055 was the one that escaped this treatement - although it was rebuilt by Willowbrook - and it was withdrawn in 1953.

Above: In 1935 a Daimler COG5SD chassis was purchased and fitted with Brush 32-seat bodywork. This single-decker, **RC 3210**, ran as No. 1208 until 1943 when it was rebodied as a double-decker with a Willowbrook utility lowbridge product. It was renumbered **1300** and was withdrawn in 1954. In this view at Derby it was parked alongside rebodied 1937 AEC Regent No. **1331** (**RC 4627**).

Below: An even more unusual vehicle was No. **1095** (**RC 5986**), also originally a single-decker (No. 507). A 1938 Daimler COG5SD, it was one of several rebodied as highbridge utility 56-seaters by Willowbrook in 1942. In 1949 it was in collision with a low bridge and had a new upper deck of unproven origin (probably ECW, but just possibly Willowbrook) fitted. The resulting vehicle is seen at Huntingdon Street in September 1950.

Above: In 1939 SOS chassis were again ordered, and of a batch of 18 SONs, 6 were bodied as 31-seat coaches and 12 as 34-seat buses, all by Willowbrook. Number **646** (**RC 7086**) was one of the coaches, seen here when brand new. *(John Banks Collection)*

Below: The same vehicle, No. **646** (**RC 7086**), was photographed at Huntingdon Street, on excursion work. This is a postwar picture, exact date unknown, by which time the vehicle had received a modified beading layout and livery. All the 1939 SONs were withdrawn in 1954.

Above: Number **644** (**RC 7084**) had, by June 1948, received a modified beading arrangement and a reversed livery of cream and red. It was at the Lawn Motor Park, Skegness. Behind was parked a postwar Windover-bodied AEC Regal III.

Below: Number **410** (**RC 7099**) was one of the 1939 SOS SON models to be bodied as 34-seat buses by Willowbrook. The vehicle was withdrawn in 1954, five years after this Huntingdon Street view was taken in September 1949. By the time of this picture the polished mouldings had been removed from the waistrail.

Above: Another example of a deteriorating negative that is nonetheless worthwhile as recording a relatively rare aspect of the fleet. Number **1058** (**RC 6007**), seen in the all-over red livery, was a 1938 Daimler COG5 with a 1946 Willowbrook highbridge body. It was withdrawn in 1957.

Below: This May 1948 photograph taken at Mount Street, Nottingham, depicts one of the 1938 Daimler COG5s that were rebodied by Brush. Number **1052** (**RC 6001**) was parked ahead of a Willowbrook-bodied Barton Leyland Titan TD7 dating from 1940.

Above: Like the rest of the rebodied 1938 Daimler COG5s, both Willowbrook and Brush examples, No. 1059 (**RC 6008**) was withdrawn in 1957. The whole batch of 14 was bought by the dealer Cowley, of Salford, and RC 6008 was sold to Cutler, trading as Lamcote Motors, of Radcliffe-on-Trent in May 1957. It then passed to Lansdowne Luxury Coaches, London E11, and was last licensed in September 1957. Less than a year, then, of further use, belied by the apparently superb condition of the vehicle in this picture of it with Lamcote Motors in June 1957.

Below: Number **1067** (**RC 7078**) was one of the 1939 Daimler COG5s to be fitted with a new Willowbrook highbridge body in 1946. It was at Derby bus station in September 1949.

Above: The wartime utility bus-building scheme, supervised by the Ministry of War Transport to specifications laid down by the Ministry of Supply, resulted in double-deckers on Guy, Daimler and Bristol chassis. Already a Daimler user, Trent was fortunate to be allocated Daimlers. Most were the CWA6 model with AEC 7.7-litre engine, which, however, was not unknown to Trent's engineers. Number **1105** (**RC 8400**) was a highbridge Roe-bodied example dating from 1944.

Below: Many wartime and immediate postwar utility bus bodies were rebuilt to keep them operational for a few more years. This 1944 Roe-bodied Trent Daimler CWA6, No. **1106** (**RC 8401**), was no exception, although Trent did less of this kind of work than many other operators. Evidence of refurbishment is particularly noticeable around the windows and the lower-deck panelling.

Above: Number **1109** (**RC 8465**) had utility bodywork by Duple, and was delivered in 1945. A highbridge 56-seater, it was photographed at Huntingon Street in apparently original structural condition and in all-over red livery.

Below: The same bus was photographed a few years later, in March 1956, at Mount Street bus station, Nottingham. Some work has obviously been done on the body, again most noticeably around the windows, especially the front upper deck ones, which now have no ventilators and are mounted in rubber moulding. This vehicle was withdrawn in 1957 and scrapped by a Manchester dealer in February of that year.

The early postwar era at Huntingdon Street bus station, Nottingham, featuring double-deckers **RC 5985** and **RC 7944**, both Daimler COG5s, the former a rebodied single-decker. The grim war years had ended and the long period of austerity and rationing was in force. Bus operators would have a golden age in the early 1950s and then face extreme difficulties brought about by mass television and car ownership, and then deregulation and privatisation. Trent is among the survivors and is still with us in 2004. Its story will continue in the companion volume *Trent 2*.